on the move

AIDS is not merely a disease, but an assault on
human dignity. We never anticipated
that once we achieved our freedom we would
face another challenge of this magnitude.
We cannot win this fight on our own, and we
rely on people like Bono to help us beat
this pandemic.

NELSON MANDELA

Inspirational words from a man of faith and
action. Bono's message is one of unparalleled
hope and challenge. He goes where others
don't and makes us want to follow.

PRESIDENT WILLIAM J. CLINTON

Few people of our day are more committed to
using their celebrity for the cause of the poor
around the world than my friend Bono, who
spoke so eloquently at the 2006 National
Prayer Breakfast.

REV. BILLY GRAHAM

A superstar of rock speaking at a National Prayer Breakfast in a Republican White House? How strange is that? Yet it's testimony to the effectiveness of Bono's campaigning to help the marginalized and the poor. Read this book and then act on it!

ARCHBISHOP DESMOND TUTU

If you would like to help us in our struggle, but you don't know how, please read this powerful book. Bono talks about complex issues but proposes some simple things to do. If enough people act, it will make a huge difference. It already has.

AGNES NYAMAYARWO, AIDS ACTIVIST, UGANDA

Bono's plea for justice, as well as charity, for those suffering from AIDS in Africa has helped change minds and hearts, as well as government policy.

SENATE MAJORITY LEADER BILL FRIST, M.D.

on the move bono

on the move bono
// a speech

W PUBLISHING GROUP
A Division of Thomas Nelson Publishers
Since 1798

on the move bono

Published by W Publishing Group,
A Division of Thomas Nelson, Inc.,
P.O. Box 141000,
Nashville, Tennessee, 37214.

W Publishing Group books may be purchased
in bulk for educational, business, fundraising,
or sales promotional use.
For information, please email
SpecialMarkets@ThomasNelson.com

All royalties earned from the sale of this book
are being donated to the ONE Campaign.
(www.one.org)

Scripture quotations are taken from
The King James Version of the Bible.

Library of Congress
Cataloging-in-Publication Data
on file

07 08 09 10 TWP 9 8 7 6 5 4 3 2 1
Printed in Singapore

THE LITTLE BOY ON PAGE 17. HE CHANGED MY LIFE.
I CAN'T REMEMBER HIS NAME.

PUBLISHER'S NOTE

THE CONTINENT OF AFRICA IS MARKED BY ITS BREATHTAKING LANDSCAPES AND RESILIENT SPIRIT. HOWEVER, HIV/AIDS IS WRECKING INCONCEIVABLE DEVASTATION ON THE COMMUNITIES OF THIS LAND. WHEN MORE THAN SIX THOUSAND LIVES ARE BEING CLAIMED EACH DAY BY THIS DEADLY DISEASE, WE CANNOT, IN GOOD CONSCIENCE, SIT BY AND WATCH.

IN OUR VIEW, NO ONE PERSON HAS SPOKEN LOUDER ON BEHALF OF THE SUFFERING THAN BONO—ROCK STAR, POET, AND VOICE OF THE VOICELESS.

HIS LEADERSHIP HAS BROUGHT ABOUT TREMENDOUS CHANGE—BILLIONS OF DOLLARS IN DEBT RELIEF HAVE BEEN FORGIVEN AND THOUSANDS OF LIVES HAVE BEEN SAVED. BUT MORE THAN THAT, HE HAS OPENED OUR EYES TO THE DIGNITY, BEAUTY, AND STRENGTH OF THIS CONTINENT. HIS ELOQUENCE WHEN SPEAKING ABOUT AFRICA AT THE NATIONAL PRAYER BREAKFAST INSPIRED THIS BOOK.

MY HOPE IS THAT IT WILL INSPIRE YOU AS WELL.

DAVID MOBERG — PUBLISHER, W PUBLISHING GROUP

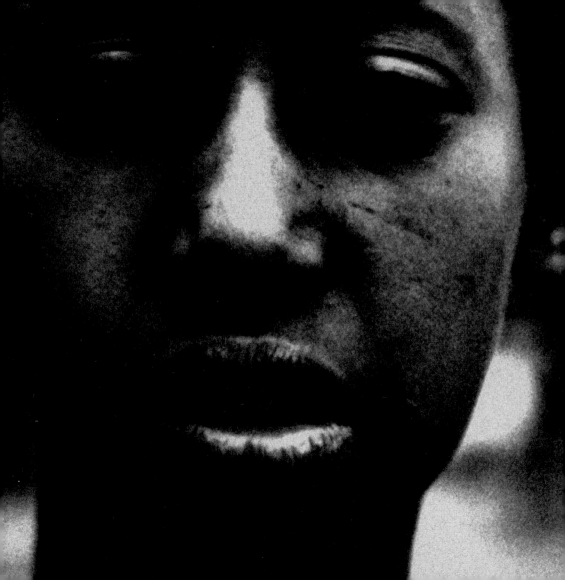

IF YOU'RE WONDERING WHAT I'M DOING HERE,

at a prayer breakfast, well, so am I. I'm certainly not here as a man of the cloth, unless that cloth is leather. And it's certainly not because I'm a rock star. Which leaves one possible explanation: I'm here because I've got a messianic complex.

Yes, it's true. And for anyone who knows me, it's hardly a revelation.

Well, I'm the first to admit that there's something unnatural . . . something unseemly . . . about rock stars mounting the pulpit and preaching at presidents, and then disappearing to their villas in the South of France. Talk about a fish out of water.

It's very humbling, and I will try to keep my homily brief.

be warned – i'm irish

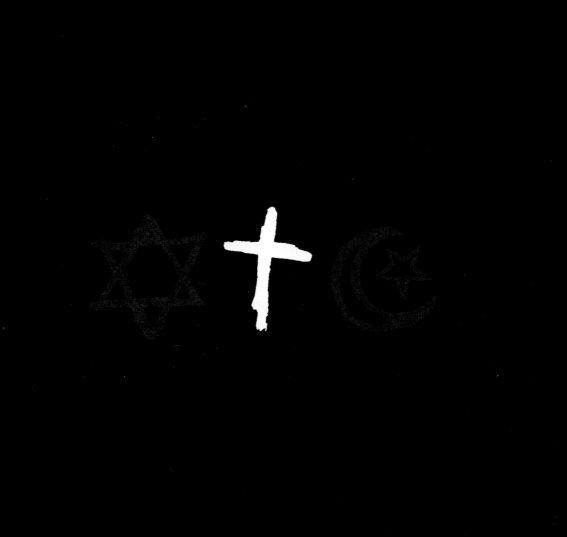

I'D LIKE TO TALK ABOUT THE LAWS OF MAN.

And I'd like to talk about higher laws. It would be great to assume that the one serves the other; that the laws of man serve these higher laws . . . but of course, they don't always. And I presume that, in a sense, is why you're here.

I presume the reason for this gathering is that all of us here—Muslims, Jews, Christians—all of us are searching our souls for how to better serve our family, our community, our nation, our God.

I know I am. Searching, I mean. And that, I suppose, is what led me here, too.

religion often gets in the way of God

YES, IT'S ODD, HAVING A ROCK STAR HERE,

but maybe it's odder for me than for you. You see, I avoided religious people most of my life. Maybe it had something to do with having a father who was Protestant and a mother who was Catholic and living in a country where the line between the two was, quite literally, a battle line—where the line between church and state was, well, a little blurry, and hard to see.

I remember how my mother would bring us to chapel on Sundays while my father used to wait outside. One of the things that I picked up from my father and my mother was the sense that religion often gets in the way of God.

For me, at least, it got in the way. Seeing what religious people, in the name of God, did to my native land . . . and in this country, America, seeing God's second-hand car salesmen on the cable TV channels, offering indulgences for cash. In fact, all over the world, seeing the self-righteousness roll down like a mighty stream from certain corners of the religious establishment.

I must confess, I changed the channel. I wanted my MTV.

I WAS CYNICAL. NOT ABOUT GOD, BUT ABOUT GOD'S POLITICS.

Then, in 1997, a couple of eccentric, septuagenarian British Christians went and ruined my shtick—my reproachfulness. They did it by describing the millennium, the year 2000, as a Jubilee year, as an opportunity to cancel the chronic debts of the world's poorest people. They had the audacity to renew the Lord's call—and they were joined by Pope John Paul II, who, from an Irish half-Catholic's point of view, may have had a more direct line to the Almighty.

"JUBILEE"—WHY "JUBILEE"?

WHAT WAS THIS YEAR OF JUBILEE, THIS YEAR OF OUR LORD'S FAVOR? I'D ALWAYS READ THE SCRIPTURES, EVEN THE OBSCURE STUFF. THERE IT WAS IN ▮▮▮▮▮▮▮▮▮. **"IF YOUR BROTHER BECOMES POOR,"** THE SCRIPTURES SAY, **"AND CANNOT MAINTAIN HIMSELF . . . YOU SHALL MAINTAIN HIM . . . YOU SHALL NOT LEND HIM YOUR MONEY AT INTEREST, NOT GIVE HIM YOUR FOOD FOR PROFIT."** IT IS SUCH AN IMPORTANT IDEA, JUBILEE, THAT JESUS BEGINS HIS MINISTRY WITH THIS. WHEN JESUS WAS A YOUNG MAN, HE MET WITH THE RABBIS, IMPRESSED EVERYONE, PEOPLE WERE TALKING. THE ELDERS SAID, "HE'S A CLEVER GUY, THIS JESUS, BUT HE HASN'T DONE MUCH . . . YET. HE HASN'T SPOKEN IN PUBLIC BEFORE . . . " WHEN HE DOES SPEAK, HIS FIRST WORDS ARE FROM ISAIAH: **"THE SPIRIT OF THE LORD IS UPON ME,"** HE SAYS, **"BECAUSE HE HAS ANOINTED ME TO PREACH GOOD NEWS TO THE POOR."** AND JESUS PROCLAIMS THE YEAR OF THE LORD'S FAVOR, THE YEAR OF JUBILEE. ▮▮▮▮▮▮▮. WHAT HE WAS REALLY TALKING ABOUT WAS AN ERA OF GRACE—AND WE'RE STILL IN IT.

SO FAST-FORWARD 2,000 YEARS.

But then my cynicism got another helping hand.

I almost started to like these church people

COLIN POWELL, A FIVE-STAR GENERAL, CALLED IT THE GREATEST W.M.D. OF THEM ALL:

a tiny little virus called AIDS. And the religious community, in large part, missed it. The ones who didn't miss it could only see it as divine retribution for bad behavior. Even on children. Even when the fastest growing group of people with HIV were married, faithful women.

Aha, there they go again! I thought to myself: Judgmentalism is back.

But in truth, I was wrong again. The church was slow, but the church got busy on this, the leprosy of our age.

Love was on the move. **Mercy** was on the move. **God** was on the move.

was on the move.   was on the move.   was on the move.

MOVING PEOPLE OF ALL KINDS

to work with others they had never met and never would have cared to meet. Conservative church groups hanging out with spokesmen for the gay community, all singing off the same hymn sheet on AIDS . . . Soccer moms and quarterbacks . . . hip-hop stars and country stars . . . This is what happens when God gets on the move: crazy stuff happens!

Popes were seen wearing sunglasses

Jesse Helms was seen with a ghetto blaster . . .

Crazy stuff! Evidence of the spirit.

It was breathtaking. Literally. It stopped the world in its tracks.

WHEN CHURCHES STARTED DEMONSTRATING ON DEBT

governments listened—and acted. When churches started organizing, petitioning, and even that most unholy of acts today, God forbid, *lobbying* on AIDS and global health, governments listened and acted.

I'm here today in all humility to say: you changed minds; you changed policy; you changed the world.

Look, whatever thoughts you have about God, who God is or if God exists —most will agree that if there is a God, God has a special place for the poor. In fact, the poor are where God lives.

Check Judaism. Check Islam. Check pretty much anyone.

I mean, God may well be with us in our mansions on the hill . . . I hope so. He may well be with us in all manner of controversial stuff . . . maybe, maybe not. But the one thing on which we can all agree, among all faiths and ideologies, is that God is with the vulnerable and poor.

You changed minds. You changed policy. You changed the world.

GOD IS IN THE SLUMS, IN THE CARDBOARD BOXES WHERE THE POOR PLAY HOUSE. GOD IS IN THE SILENCE OF A MOTHER WHO HAS INFECTED HER CHILD WITH A VIRUS THAT WILL END BOTH THEIR LIVES. GOD IS IN THE CRIES HEARD UNDER THE RUBBLE OF WAR. GOD IS IN THE DEBRIS OF WASTED OPPORTUNITY AND LIVES, AND **GOD IS WITH US IF WE ARE WITH THEM.** "IF YOU REMOVE THE YOKE FROM YOUR MIDST, THE POINTIN

OF THE FINGER AND SPEAKING WICKEDNESS, AND IF YOU GIVE YOURSELF TO THE HUNGRY AND SATISFY THE DESIRE OF THE AFFLICTED, THEN YOUR LIGHT WILL RISE IN DARKNESS AND YOUR GLOOM WILL BECOME LIKE MIDDAY AND THE LORD WILL CONTINUALLY GUIDE YOU AND SATISFY YOUR DESIRE IN SCORCHED PLACES" (ISAIAH 58:9-11).

IT'S NOT A COINCIDENCE

that in the Scriptures, poverty is mentioned more than 2,100 times. It's not an accident. That's a lot of airtime, 2,100 mentions.

You know, the only time Christ is judgmental is on the subject of the poor. "As you have done it unto the least of these my brethren, you have done it unto me" (Matthew 25:40). As I say, good news to the poor.

And here's some good news for the President. After 9-11 we were told America would have no time for the world's poor. America would be taken up with its own problems of safety. And it's true these are dangerous times, but America has not drawn the blinds and double-locked the doors.

In fact, America has doubled aid to Africa. America has tripled funding for global health. The President's Emergency Plan for AIDS Relief, and support, with Congress, for the Global Fund has put 900,000 people onto life-saving anti-retroviral drugs and provided eleven million bed nets to protect children from malaria.

Outstanding human achievements. Counterintuitive. Historic. Be very, very proud.

BUT HERE'S THE BAD NEWS.

There is much more to do. There's a gigantic chasm between the scale of the emergency and the scale of the response.

And finally, it's not about charity after all, is it? It's about justice.

Let me repeat that: It's not about charity. It's about justice.

And that's too bad.

Because you're good at charity. Americans, like the Irish, are good at it. We like to give, and we give a lot, even those who can't afford it.

But justice is a higher standard. Africa makes a fool of our idea of justice. It makes a farce of our idea of equality. It mocks our pieties; it doubts our concern; it questions our commitment.

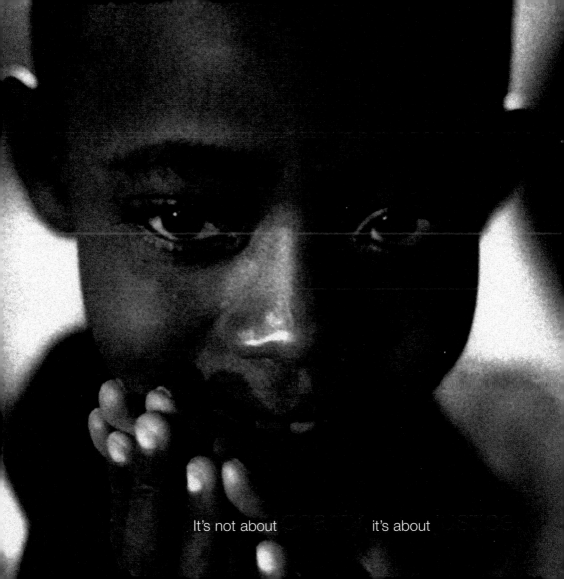

It's not about   it's about

It's a completely avoidable catastrophe.

6,500 AFRICANS ARE STILL DYING EVERY DAY

of a preventable, treatable disease, for lack of drugs we can buy at any drugstore. This is not about charity; this is about justice and equality.

Because there's no way we can look at what's happening in Africa and, if we're honest, conclude that deep down, we really accept that Africans are equal to us. Anywhere else in the world, we wouldn't accept it. Look at what happened in Southeast Asia with the Tsunami. 150,000 lives lost to that misnomer of all misnomers, "mother nature." In Africa 150,000 lives are lost every month. A tsunami every month. And it's a completely avoidable catastrophe.

It's annoying, but justice and equality are mates. Aren't they? Justice always wants to hang out with equality. And equality is a *real pain.*

YOU KNOW, THINK OF THOSE
JEWISH SHEEP-HERDERS

going to meet the Pharaoh, mud on their shoes, and the Pharaoh says, "Equal?" A preposterous idea: rich and poor are equal? And they say, "Yeah, 'equal,' that's what it says here in this book. We're all made in the image of God."

And eventually the Pharaoh says, "Okay, I can accept that. I can accept the Jews—but not the blacks.

"Not the women. Not the gays. Not the Irish. No way, man."

So on we go with our journey of equality.

On we go in the pursuit of justice.

where you *live* should no longer determine *whether* you live

WE HEAR THAT CALL IN THE ONE CAMPAIGN,

a growing movement of more than two million Americans . . . left and right together, united in the belief that *where* you live should no longer determine *whether* you live.

Preventing the poorest of the poor from selling their products while we sing the virtues of the free market—that's a justice issue. Holding children ransom for the debts of their grandparents—that's a justice issue. Withholding life-saving medicines out of deference to the Office of Patents—that's a justice issue. And while the law is what we say it is, God is not silent on the subject.

THAT'S WHY I SAY THERE'S THE LAW OF THE LAND,

and then there is a higher standard. We can hire experts to write the laws of the land so that they benefit us. So, the laws say it's okay to protect our agriculture but it's not okay for African farmers to do the same, to earn a living?

As the laws of man are written, that's what they say.

God will not accept that.

Mine won't, at least. Will yours?

it's okay to   our   ~~griculture~~
but it's not okay for african farmers to do the same

THIS IS A DANGEROUS IDEA I'VE PUT ON THE TABLE: **MY GOD VS. YOUR GOD, THEIR GOD VS. OUR GOD … VS. NO GOD.** IT IS VERY EASY, IN THESE TIMES, TO SEE RELIGION AS A FORCE FOR DIVISION RATHER THAN UNITY. THE REASON I AM HERE IN WASHINGTON, AND THE REASON I KEEP COMING BACK, IS BECAUSE THIS IS A TOWN THAT IS PROVING IT

CAN COME TOGETHER ON BEHALF OF WHO THE SCRIPTURES CALL "THE LEAST OF THESE."

THIS IS NOT A REPUBLICAN IDEA. IT IS NOT A DEMOCRATIC IDEA. IT IS NOT EVEN, WITH ALL DUE RESPECT, AN AMERICAN IDEA. NOR IT IS UNIQUE TO ANY ONE FAITH.

"DO TO OTHERS AS YOU WOULD HAVE THEM DO TO YOU" (LUKE 6:31). JESUS SAYS THAT.

"RIGHTEOUSNESS IS THIS: THAT ONE SHOULD . . . GIVE AWAY WEALTH OUT OF LOVE FOR HIM TO THE NEAR OF KIN AND THE ORPHANS AND THE NEEDY AND THE WAYFARER AND THE BEGGARS AND FOR THE EMANCIPATION OF THE CAPTIVES" (2:177). THE KORAN SAYS THAT.

THUS SAYETH THE LORD: **"BRING THE HOMELESS POOR INTO THE HOUSE, WHEN YOU SEE THE NAKED, COVER HIM, THEN YOUR LIGHT WILL BREAK OUT LIKE THE DAWN AND YOUR RECOVERY WILL SPEEDILY SPRING FORTH, THEN YOUR LORD WILL BE YOUR REAR GUARD."** THE JEWISH SCRIPTURE SAYS THAT. ISAIAH 58 AGAIN.

THAT IS A POWERFUL INCENTIVE: "THE LORD WILL WATCH YOUR BACK." SOUNDS LIKE A GOOD DEAL TO ME, RIGHT NOW.

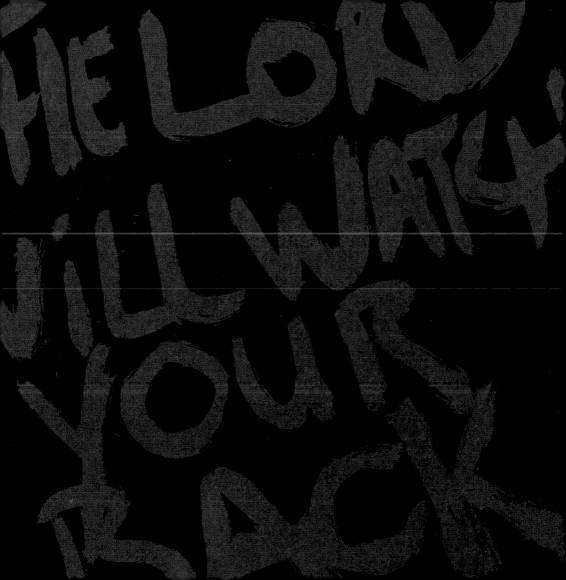

A NUMBER OF YEARS AGO, I MET A WISE MAN

who changed my life. In countless ways, large and small, I was always seeking the Lord's blessing. I was saying, you know, "I have a new song, look after it." Or, "I have a family, please look after them." Or, "I have this crazy idea . . . "

And this wise man said: "Stop." He said, "Stop asking God to bless what you're doing. Get involved in what God is doing—because it's already blessed."

Well, God, as I said, is with the poor. That, I believe, is what God is doing. And that is what He's calling us to do.

WHEN I FIRST GOT TO AMERICA

and I learned how much some church-goers tithe. Some tithe up to ten percent of the family budget. Well, how does that compare with the federal budget, the budget for the entire American family? How much of that goes to the poorest people in the world? **Less than one percent.**

I want to suggest to you today that you see the flow of effective foreign assistance as tithing . . . Which, to be truly meaningful, will mean an additional one percent of the federal budget tithed to the poor.

is the girl in Africa who gets to go to school

WHAT IS ONE PERCENT?

One percent is not merely a number on a balance sheet.

One percent is the girl in Africa who gets to go to school—thanks to you. One percent is the AIDS patient who gets her medicine—thanks to you. One percent is the African entrepreneur who can start a small family business—thanks to you. One percent is not redecorating presidential palaces or money flowing down a rat hole. This one percent is digging waterholes to provide clean water.

ONE PERCENT IS A NEW PARTNERSHIP WITH AFRICA,

not paternalism toward Africa, where increased assistance flows toward improved governance and initiatives with proven track records—away from boondoggles and white elephants of every description.

America gives less than one percent now. We're asking for an extra one percent to change the world. This will not only transform the lives of millions of people—and I say this to the military men now—it will also transform the way those people see us.

One percent is national security, enlightened economic self-interest, and a better, safer world rolled into one. Sounds to me that in this town of deals and compromises,

one percent is the best bargain around.

THESE GOALS—CLEAN WATER FOR ALL,

school for every child, medicine for the afflicted, an end to extreme and senseless poverty—these are not just any goals; they are the Millennium Development goals, which this country, America, supports. And they are more than that:

They are the Beatitudes for a Globalized World

NOW, I'M VERY LUCKY.

I don't have to sit on any budget committees. And I certainly don't have to sit where you do, Mr. President. I don't have to make the tough choices.

To give one percent
more is right. It's smart. And it's blessed.

THERE IS A CONTINENT—**AFRICA**
—BEING CONSUMED BY FLAMES.

I TRULY BELIEVE THAT WHEN THE
HISTORY BOOKS ARE WRITTEN, OUR
AGE WILL BE REMEMBERED FOR
THREE THINGS: THE WAR ON
TERROR, THE DIGITAL REVOLUTION,
AND WHAT WE DID—OR DID
NOT DO—TO PUT THE FIRE OUT
IN AFRICA.

HISTORY, LIKE GOD,
IS WATCHING WHAT WE DO >

on the move bono

If you're wondering what I'm doing here, at a prayer breakfast, well, so am I. I'm certainly not here as a man of the cloth, unless that cloth is leather. And, it's certainly not because I'm a rock star. Which leaves one possible explanation: I'm here because I've got a messianic complex. Yes, it's true. And for anyone who knows me, it's hardly a revelation.

Well, I'm the first to admit that there's something unnatural . . . perhaps something unseemly . . . about rock stars mounting the pulpit and preaching at presidents, and then disappearing to their villas in the South of France. Talk about a fish out of water. It's very humbling, and I will try to keep my homily brief. But be warned—I'm Irish.

I'd like to talk about the laws of man. And I'd like to talk about higher laws. It would be great to assume that the one serves the other; that the laws of man serve these higher laws . . . but of course, they don't always. And I presume that, in a sense, is why you're here.

I presume the reason for this gathering is that all of us here—Muslims, Jews, Christians—all of us are searching our souls for how to better serve our family, our community, our nation, our God.

I know I am. Searching, I mean. And that, I suppose, is what led me here, too.

Yes, it's odd, having a rock star here, but maybe it's odder for me than for you. You see, I avoided religious people most of my life. Maybe it had something to do with having a father who was Protestant and a mother who was Catholic and living in a country where the line between the two was, quite literally, a battle line—where the line between church and state was, well, a little blurry, and hard to see.

I remember how my mother would bring us to chapel on Sundays while my father used to wait outside. One of the things that I picked up from my father and my mother was the sense that religion often gets in the way of God.

For me, at least, it got in the way. Seeing what religious people, in the name of God, did to my native land . . . and in this country, America, seeing God's second-hand car salesmen on the cable TV channels, offering indulgences for cash. In fact, all over the world, seeing the self-righteousness roll down like a mighty stream from certain corners of the religious establishment.

I must confess, I changed the channel. I wanted my MTV. Even though I was a believer. Perhaps because I was a believer.

I was cynical. Not about God, but about God's politics. Then, in 1997, a couple of eccentric, septuagenarian British Christians went and ruined my shtick—my reproachfulness. They did it by describing the millennium, the year 2000, as a Jubilee year, as an opportunity to cancel the chronic debts of the world's poorest people. They had the audacity to renew the Lord's call—and they were joined by Pope John Paul II, who, from an Irish half-Catholic's point of view, may have had a more direct line to the Almighty.

"Jubilee"—why "Jubilee"?

What was this year of Jubilee, this year of our Lord's favor? I'd always read the Scriptures, even the obscure stuff. There it was in Leviticus [25:35] . . . "If your brother becomes poor," the Scriptures say, "and cannot maintain himself . . . you shall maintain him . . . You shall not lend him your money at interest, not give him your food for profit."

It is such an important idea, Jubilee, that Jesus begins his ministry with this. When Jesus was a young man, he met with the rabbis, impressed everyone, people were talking. The elders said, "He's a clever guy, this Jesus, but he hasn't done much . . . yet. He hasn't spoken in public before . . ."

When he does speak, his first words are from Isaiah: "The Spirit of the Lord is upon me," he says, "because He has anointed me to preach good news to the poor." And Jesus proclaims the year of the Lord's favor, the year of Jubilee. (Luke 4:18)

What he was really talking about was an era of grace—and we're still in it.

So fast-forward 2,000 years. That same thought, grace, was made incarnate— in a movement of all kinds of people. The Jubilee movement wasn't a bless-me club; it wasn't a holy huddle. These religious guys were willing to get out in the streets, get their boots dirty, wave the placards, follow their convictions with actions. Making it really hard for people like me to keep their distance.

It was amazing. I almost started to like these church people.

But then my cynicism got another helping hand.

Colin Powell, a five-star general, called it the greatest W.M.D. of them all: a tiny little virus called AIDS. And the religious community, in large part, missed it. The ones who didn't miss it could only see it as divine retribution for bad behavior. Even on children. Even when the fastest growing group of people with HIV were married, faithful women.

Aha, there they go again! I thought to myself: Judgmentalism is back.

But in truth, I was wrong again. The church was slow, but the church got busy on this, the leprosy of our age.

Love was on the move. *Mercy* was on the move. *God* was on the move.

Moving people of all kinds to work with others they had never met and never would have cared to meet.

Conservative church groups hanging out with spokesmen for the gay community, all singing off the same hymn sheet on AIDS . . . Soccer moms and quarterbacks . . . hip-hop stars and country stars . . . This is what happens when God gets on the move: crazy stuff happens!

Popes were seen wearing sunglasses . . .

Jesse Helms was seen with a ghetto blaster . . .

Crazy stuff. Evidence of the Spirit.

It was breathtaking. Literally. It stopped the world in its tracks.

When churches started demonstrating on debt governments listened—and acted. When churches starting organizing, petitioning, and even that most unholy of acts today, God forbid, *lobbying* on AIDS and global health, governments listened, and acted.

I'm here today in all humility to say: you changed minds; you changed policy; you changed the world.

Look, whatever thoughts you have about God, who God is or if God exists—most will agree that if there is a God, God has a special place for the poor.

In fact, the poor are where God lives.

Check Judaism. Check Islam. Check pretty much anyone.

I mean, God may well be with us in our mansions on the hill . . . I hope so. He may well be with us in all manner of controversial stuff . . . maybe, maybe not. But the one thing on which we can all agree, among all faiths and ideologies, is that God is with the vulnerable and poor.

God is in the slums, in the cardboard boxes where the poor play house. God is in the silence of a mother who has infected her child with a virus that will end both their lives. God is in the cries heard under the rubble of war. God is in the debris of wasted opportunity and lives, and God is with us if we are with them. "If you remove the yoke from your midst, the pointing of the finger and speaking wickedness, and if you give yourself to the hungry and satisfy the desire of the afflicted, then your light will rise in darkness and your gloom will become like midday and the Lord will continually guide you and satisfy your desire in scorched places" (Isaiah 58:9-11).

It's not a coincidence that in the Scriptures, poverty is mentioned more than 2,100 times. It's not an accident. That's a lot of airtime, 2,100 mentions.

You know, the only time Christ is judgmental is on the subject of the poor. "As you have done it unto the least of these my brethren, you have done it unto me" (Matthew 25:40). As I say, good news to the poor.

And here's some good news for the President. After 9-11 we were told America would have no time for the world's poor. America would be taken up with its own problems of safety. And it's true these are dangerous times, but America has not drawn the blinds and double-locked the doors.

In fact, America has doubled aid to Africa. America has tripled funding for global health. The President's Emergency Plan for AIDS Relief, and support, with Congress, for the Global Fund has put 900,000 people onto life-saving anti-retroviral drugs and provided eleven million bed nets to protect children from malaria.

Outstanding human achievements. Counterintuitive. Historic. Be very, very proud.

But here's the bad news. There is much more to do. There's a gigantic chasm between the scale of emergency and the scale of response. And finally, it's not about charity after all, is it? It's about justice.

Let me repeat that: It's not about charity. It's about justice.

And that's too bad. Because you're good at charity. Americans, like the Irish, are good at it. We like to give, and we give a lot, even those who can't afford it.

But justice is a higher standard. Africa makes a fool of our idea of justice. It makes a farce of our idea of equality. It mocks our pieties; it doubts our concern; and it questions our commitment.

6,500 Africans are still dying every day of a preventable, treatable disease, for lack of drugs we can buy at any drugstore. This is not about charity; this is about justice and equality.

Because there's no way we can look at what's happening in Africa and, if we're honest, conclude that deep down, we really accept that Africans are equal to us. Anywhere else in the world, we wouldn't accept it. Look at what happened in Southeast Asia with the Tsunami. 150,000 lives lost to that misnomer of all misnomers, "mother nature." In Africa, 150,000 lives are lost every month. A tsunami every month. And it's a completely avoidable catastrophe.

It's annoying, but justice and equality are mates. Aren't they? Justice always wants to hang out with equality. And equality is a *real pain.*

You know, think of those Jewish sheep-herders going to meet the Pharaoh, mud on their shoes, and the Pharaoh says, "Equal?" A preposterous idea: rich and poor are equal? And they say, "Yeah, 'equal,' that's what it says here in this book. We're all made in the image of God."

And eventually the Pharaoh says, "Okay, I can accept that. I can accept the Jews—but not the blacks. Not the women. Not the gays. Not the Irish. No way, man."

So on we go with our journey of equality. On we go in the pursuit of justice.

We hear that call in the ONE Campaign, a growing movement of more than two million Americans . . . left and right together, united in the belief that *where* you live should no longer determine *whether* you live.

Preventing the poorest of the poor from selling their products while we sing the virtues of the free market—that's a justice issue. Holding children ransom for the debts of their grandparents—that's a justice issue. Withholding life-saving medicines out of deference to the Office of Patents—that's a justice issue. And while the law is what we say it is, God is not silent on the subject.

That's why I say there's the law of the land, and then there is a higher standard. We can hire experts to write the laws of the land so that they benefit us. So, the laws say it's okay to protect our agriculture but it's not okay for African farmers to do the same, to earn a living?

As the laws of man are written, that's what they say.

God will not accept that.

Mine won't, at least. Will yours?

This is a dangerous idea I've put on the table: my God vs. your God, their God vs. our God . . . vs. no God. It is very easy, in these times, to see religion as a force for division rather than unity. The reason I am here in Washington, and the reason I keep coming back, is because this is a town that is proving it can come together on behalf of who the Scriptures call "the least of these."

This is not a Republican idea. It is not a Democratic idea. It is not even, with all due respect, an American idea. Nor it is unique to any one faith.

"Do to others as you would have them do to you" (Luke 6:31). Jesus says that.

"Righteousness is this: that one should . . . give away wealth out of love for Him to the near of kin and the orphans and the needy and the wayfarer and the beggars and for the emancipation of the captives" (2.177). The Koran says that.

Thus sayeth the Lord: "Bring the homeless poor into the house, when you

see the naked, cover him, then your light will break out like the dawn and your recovery will speedily spring forth, then your Lord will be your rear guard."
The Jewish Scripture says that.
Isaiah 58 again.

That is a powerful incentive: "The Lord will watch your back." Sounds like a good deal to me, right now.

A number of years ago, I met a wise man who changed my life. In countless ways, large and small, I was always seeking the Lord's blessing. I was saying, you know, "I have a new song, look after it." Or, "I have a family, please look after them." Or, "I have this crazy idea . . ."

And this wise man said: "Stop." He said, "Stop asking God to bless what you're doing. Get involved in what God is doing—because it's already blessed."

Well, God, as I said, is with the poor. That, I believe, is what God is doing. And that is what He's calling us to do.

I was amazed when I first got to America and I learned how much some church-goers tithe. Some tithe up to ten percent of the family budget. Well, how does that compare with the federal budget, the budget for the entire American family? How much of that goes to the poorest people in the world? Less than one percent.

I want to suggest to you today that you see the flow of effective foreign assistance as tithing . . . Which, to be truly meaningful, will mean an additional one percent of the federal budget tithed to the poor.

What is one percent?

One percent is not merely a number on a balance sheet.

One percent is the girl in Africa who gets to go to school—thanks to you. One percent is the AIDS patient who gets her medicine—thanks to you. One percent is the African entrepreneur who can start a small family business—thanks to you. One percent is not redecorating presidential palaces or money flowing down a rat hole. This one percent is digging waterholes to provide clean water.

One percent is a new partnership with Africa, not paternalism toward Africa, where increased assistance flows toward improved governance and initiatives with proven track records—away from boondoggles and white elephants of every description.

America gives less than one percent now. We're asking for an extra one percent to change the world. This will not only transform the lives of millions of people— and I say this to the military men now—it will also transform the way those people see us.

One percent is national security, enlightened economic self-interest, and a better, safer world rolled into one. Sounds to me that in this town of deals and compromises, one percent is the best bargain around.

These goals—clean water for all, school for every child, medicine for the afflicted, an end to extreme and senseless poverty—these are not just any goals; they are the Millennium Development goals, which this country, America, supports. And they are more than that: They are the Beatitudes for a Globalized World.

Now, I'm very lucky. I don't have to sit on any budget committees. And, I certainly

don't have to sit where you do, Mr. President. I don't have to make the tough choices.

But I can tell you this: To give one percent more is right. It's smart. And it's blessed.

There is a continent—Africa—being consumed by flames.

I truly believe that when the history books are written, our age will be remembered for three things: the war on terror, the digital revolution, and what we did—or did not do—to put the fire out in Africa.

History, like God, is watching what we do.

ONE

THE CAMPAIGN TO MAKE
POVERTY HISTORY
WWW.ONE.ORG

The ONE Campaign is a grassroots movement of groups and individuals working together to rally students and soccer moms, punk rockers and preachers, Americans from every walk—ONE by ONE—to fight the emergency of global AIDS and extreme poverty.

To date, more than 2.4 million Americans have signed the ONE declaration at www.one.org. Thousands more are joining every day. Our goal is to reach more than five million members by 2008, making the fight against global AIDS and extreme poverty a top priority for U.S. presidential candidates.

ONE believes that allocating an additional 1 percent of the US budget toward basic needs in the poorest countries—like health, education, clean water, and food—would transform the futures and hopes of an entire generation who currently survive on less than a dollar a day. ONE also calls for debt cancellation, trade reform, and anti–corruption measures in a comprehensive package to help Africa and the world's poorest nations beat AIDS and extreme poverty.

After you join by signing the declaration, wear the ONE white wristband to show your support. Read more about the poorest countries on ONE.org. Tell your friends and family about ONE and encourage them to join. Attend local ONE events in your area. Let your representatives in Washington know what you think they could do to combat extreme poverty. Take part in ONE's email campaigns. Write about ONE on your blog. Talk about ONE on your podcast. Host a banner on your website. Host a prayer meeting in your church. Host a party in your house.

These are just a few ideas of how you can help in the fight against AIDS and extreme poverty. The scale of the challenge can feel overwhelming, but it's amazing how much difference one person can make when everyone takes action together. PLEASE JOIN US.

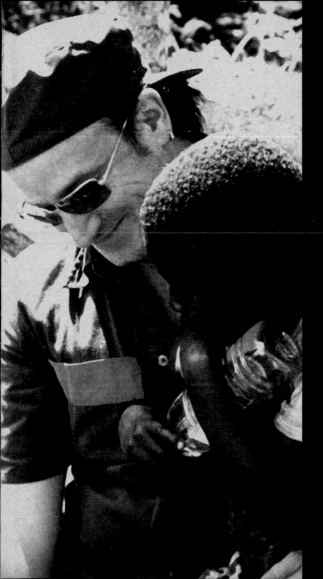

ACKNOWLEDGMENTS

I want to thank my editors,
Lucy, Jeff and everyone at **DATA.**

ABOUT THE AUTHOR

Bono is the lead singer of Irish rock
group U2. In 2002, he co-founded
the advocacy group **DATA**
(Debt, AIDS, Trade, Africa) which is
a member of One, the Campaign to
Make Poverty History (www.one.org)
In 2006 he launched Product (RED)
to engage businesses in the fight
against AIDS. Bono lives in Dublin
with his wife and four children.

ETHIOPIAN PORTRAITS
Bono

FRONT COVER IMAGE
Bono

PHOTOS OF AUTHOR
Kevin Davies

ART DIRECTION
Steve Averill

DESIGN
Gary Kelly - FOUR5ONE CREATIVE